A Mississippi Family

The Griffins of Magnolia Terrace, Griffin's Refuge, and Greenville 1800-1950

Mary Helen Griffin Halloran

iUniverse, Inc.
New York   Bloomington

A Mississippi Family
The Griffins of Magnolia Terrace, Griffin's
Refuge, and Greenville 1800-1950

The views expressed in this work are solely those of the author and do not necessarily reflect the views of the publisher, and the publisher hereby disclaims any responsibility for them.

iUniverse books may be ordered through booksellers or by contacting:

iUniverse
1663 Liberty Drive
Bloomington, IN 47403
www.iuniverse.com
1-800-Authors (1-800-288-4677)

Because of the dynamic nature of the Internet, any Web addresses or links contained in this book may have changed since publication and may no longer be valid.

ISBN: 978-1-4401-4222-2 (sc)
ISBN: 978-1-4401-4223-9 (dj)
ISBN: 978-1-4401-4224-6 (ebk)

Printed in the United States of America

iUniverse rev. date: 5/28/2009

FOR MY CHILDREN
AND THEIR CHILDREN
AND THEIRS

Contents

INTRODUCTION

We never know when the impulse to write a family history will ambush us from an unexpected direction. I grew up in Mississippi and aged into a vague nagging shame about my heritage. I was not inclined to explore roots that dug into the "most southern place on earth" about which James Cobb, a distinguished American historian, remarked:

> Behind the seductive and disarming Old South facade of the Mississippi Delta, the American Dream has been not so much perverted as simply pursued to its ultimate realization in a setting where human and natural resources have been exploited to the fullest, but without regard for social or institutional restraints. ... [Here] the pursuit of wealth, pleasure and power overwhelm the ideals of equality, justice, and compassion and reduce the American Dream to a self-indulgent fantasy (Cobb 1992, 326).

As I grew more aware of the shadow race cast across the community I grew up in, the more interested I became in the history of my mother's Sheldon family. After joining the California Gold Rush, they left Vermont to settle in Nebraska far from the extended family that had surrounded and supported them for five generations. From them I inherited a length of homespun checked red and blue and the legend of a woman who fired up her oven to bake loaves of bread for Indian squaws. I imagined her as the true pioneer and that family a true success story since my mother's father, my grandfather, having earned a degree at Harvard and joined Teddy Roosevelt and his Rough Riders in Cuba, served a term as Governor of Nebraska before moving his family to Mississippi.

Slowly I became more curious about my father's Griffin ancestors who traveled over the mountains of the western Carolinas, down the tributaries of the Tennessee, the Cumberland, onto the Ohio River, and finally to the Yazoo-Mississippi Delta. The rivers they navigated flowed southwest and south. Before the invention of steam-powered boats, flatboats were the arks of discovery on one-way trips down river to become building material or steamboat fuel at the end of the journey. Not long after Daniel Boone opened the Wilderness Road into Kentucky, Jonas and Janet Bettis Griffin flat boated through a wilderness—with five children, some livestock and house furnishings—to the new Mississippi frontier troubled by Indians, outlaws, border disputes, and shady land agents. Just after the turn of the nineteenth century, they reached their destination, a large plat of land near Vicksburg, Mississippi claimed by Jonas in 1797. They cleared swamp, built levees, and coped with malaria, yellow fever, typhoid, and tuberculosis and watched their neighbors die.

The Griffin family came to what became Warren County in 1800, resettled in Washington County in 1828, and moved to the town of Greenville in 1879. Since the Sheldons had not arrived in the Mississippi Delta until the first decade of the twentieth century, I grew up with the uneasy feeling of being half a foreigner in a community where many families, including half of mine, had lived for five generations. I was troubled by the knowledge that the Griffins had owned slaves while the Sheldons had smuggled them to freedom. My hand-me-down wardrobe signaled that both halves of my family had skidded down the ladder of economic success.

Like many of my friends, I left my hometown—its values, virtues, and vices—to live outside the South. I happily entered the academic world where merit, brains, and ability—not family—shape success. I taught contentedly for more than thirty years. My thoughts about family shrank to a concern for my own children, my nieces and nephews, and my husband's parents. My concern was the immediate present and the future. I left the past behind.

In the end, of course, we never escape our past. As I neared retirement, with some trepidation, I opened a manuscript that had skulked in a saltine box, wrapped in tissue paper, in the farthest corners of the top shelves of my closets in the several houses I inhabited for fifty years. According to family lore the box contained the manuscript of an epic poem about Napoleon called "In Ruin Robed" which my great-grandfather Judge John Bettis Griffin wrote after he moved to town from the old plantation. When I opened the box, I found 180 pages of oversized unlined ledger paper with meticulous handwriting on both sides. It was not an epic poem at all, but a romance about pirates set in eighteenth century Florida. In the tale, virtuous English and Irish privateers commissioned by the Spanish king prey on the unscrupulous British navy. It contains long tall tales in dialect— Negro (think Uncle Remus) and Irish (think William Carleton). Its villains are named for the local superintendent of schools in Greenville, Mississippi, and that state's U. S. Senator at the turn of the century. Its heroes bear the nicknames of neighbors fancied up into mock Spanish, and its heroine is named after the writer's daughter-in-law, my grandmother, Corinne Urquhart Griffin.

Transcribing spidery brown Palmer script into a readable word processor document proved to be the perfect daytime task for my six-month sojourn in Abu Dhabi in the United Arab Emirates.

The more I transcribed, the more convinced I became that I had a window into the mind of my great-grandfather, a story teller of great charm who held the neighborhood children spell-bound on summer evenings with tales of Mike Flanagan, one of the manuscript's colorful characters who frequently sought the help of the " Mither of God "and "sweet Jaysus."

While the manuscript substantiated family legend about Judge Griffin's story-telling ability, it was not a single well-formed narrative, but a succession of tales, some based on fact, some purely imaginary, strung together on a loose narrative thread. The document provided psychological and sociological insight into the mind and times of my great-grandfather. The best literary parts are lively tales in dialect, baby talk, or the voice of a fool, Charleth Thimpthon, who stutters through a long defense of dueling with every ess-sound the story teller could work in. These sections were clearly designed to be recited with voice changes and hand gestures.

In the duller patches, I learned how my great-grandfather would lay out an ideal plantation, how he would design a house and landscape its grounds, how he felt about slavery, love in old age, and strong women. In one comic episode, Miss Hetty drives off armed bandits with a horsewhip and then turns to assure her stuttering escort he had saved the day. A long ghost story is embedded in a vignette about young children going from the big house to the slave quarters after supper to listen to a story. The doings of "Limpin Aily wid de winkin light" and a detailed picture of a pirate's hideout are the stuff to enthrall children. I imagined gatherings after dinner on the porch of the house on South Broadway where in a rocker, or a porch swing sat my Great-grandfather John Griffin telling, in different voices and inflections, a four-page tale to eight or nine children lounging on the steps I began to ponder how he produced the week's allotted pages. Did he write them down in advance like a preacher writing a sermon? Or did he commit the story to paper later to preserve it for another telling? Or did he write simply to remind himself where to begin next week's installment?

I had transcribed a manuscript and developed a theory about how it was produced, but I did not know what to do with it. I congratulated myself, nonetheless, on knowing more about my great-grandfather who died in 1903 than my father knew—than, indeed, any of my living relatives knew. John Griffin's carefully preserved manuscript was not a Napoleonic epic. Its progenitors were not *Paradise Lost* or the romances of Sir Walter Scott, but the *Pickwick Papers* of Dickens. It emerged from the oral story-telling tradition practiced in print by Mark Twain at the end of the nineteenth century and continued more than a hundred years later by Garrison Keillor's *News from Lake Wobegon.*

I had tried to put the past aside, but it did not stay put. I found myself with a grandchild who wanted to know the history of her name. A niece wrote to find out about both her grandmother and the great-grandmother for whom she was named. So when I went home to Greenville for my forty-fifth high school reunion, I went to the library and looked up some hundred-year-old newspapers. I had received pictures of a sadly neglected family graveyard on Refuge, the old Griffin plantation south of Greenville. My cousin Anson Sheldon, who lives on a plantation not far from Refuge, drove me through cotton fields to the abandoned Griffin Cemetery. It was marked by a single bedraggled tree surrounded by abandoned farm and drainage equipment and a few tombstones half buried in the dirt. I decided to hire an excavation company to clean it up and move the surviving Refuge grave markers into Griffin family plots in the Greenville Cemetery where they could be preserved. I knew that my great-great-grandfather, Francis Griffin, who settled and built Griffin's Refuge, had asked to be buried in an unmarked grave on his land surrounded by the Negroes who had made his fortune. I spotted a glass jar with fresh flowers, and it dawned on me that for some in the neighborhood that ground remained sacred. Suddenly I was knee-deep in Mississippi history.

The writer of a family history who finds a bundle of letters, a scrapbook, or a journal from which to spin a narrative is lucky. My Griffin family is short on that kind of evidence. For a glimpse into the family's participation in the society of the Old South cotton plantation era, I have relied on family tradition as recorded in 1950 by Lydia Stockman Griffin Trenholm (1888–1960). Aunt Mitten, as I called her, was my father's first cousin who grew up with him in their grandfather Judge John Bettis Griffin's busy and crowded house on South Broadway in Greenville. "Mitten's Chronicle" captures the locally preferred of two competing myths about the earliest settlers of Washington County. She peopled her history with the younger sons of gentlemen from Virginia and South Carolina coming into the area with slaves and wealth to dot—almost overnight—the flat rich delta land with magnolia-scented, moonlit plantations. My father's sister Sarah Lane Griffin Shackelford, herself a wonderful story teller, celebrated rogues, gamblers, and dirt-poor farmers draining swamps, driving mules, growing cotton, marrying money, and gaining respectability.

Mitten's "Chronicle" gave me an outline. Books about the early south-westward movement immediately after the American Revolution allowed me to piece together a version of the Griffins' early travels. Judge John Griffin's pirate romance painted an idealized picture of life on Refuge plantation during the 1830s. The account book for Refuge Plantation between 1855 and 1861 accorded me a blurred glimpse of plantation business and the lives of Refuge slaves. In the 1880s and 1890s Griffin names began to appear in the local newspapers and other written records of the time. I have supplemented my three primary sources with records now available on the Internet and many years of Greenville newspapers—the *Greenville Times,* the *Democrat,* and the *Delta Democrat Times.* These sources provide a skeleton of the life of the Griffin clan of Washington County for 130 years.

I have fleshed out that skeleton with other published sources. Papers of the Washington County Historical Society and the Mississippi Historical Society have yielded anecdotes about my great-grandfather Judge John Griffin, his father Francis, and his grandfather Jonas, the original Mississippi settler. Dunbar Rowland's various accounts of Mississippi history provided some details about their public lives. By far the most entertaining and useful source was Goodspeed's *Biographical and Historical Memoirs of Mississippi: Embracing an Authentic and Comprehensive Account of the Chief Events in the State and a Record of the Lives of Many of the Most Worthy and Illustrious Families and Individuals.* This four-volume tome (twenty-five-hundred pages) printed in Chicago in 1890 enabled me to reconstruct the network of neighbors that surrounded the Griffins on Refuge Plantation between 1827 and 1860. A number of these neighbors kept journals and diaries that have found their way into the collections of libraries and archives, and from there into academic books where they enliven history about Warren and Washington Counties and the Mississippi Delta.

When I began my task, my goal was to write a family book, to raise the bones of the ancestors and make them live for the seventh generation of Griffins now scattered across the East, South, and West of our country. As I explored records, maps and account books to solve family mysteries, I came to appreciate how poring over probate records and tax lists can help recreate neighborhoods and tease out courtship patterns. Griffin men dominate the early years because only their names appear on tax lists, land claims, and early Federal Census records. I have set the stage for Griffin lives by summarizing the findings of contemporary historians about Mississippi law, honor, slavery, and the technology and business of cotton culture. I have painted a backdrop to the life the family lived once it settled in Greenville with a smorgasbord of the contents and advertising of several Greenville newspapers between 1870 and 1910. Finally, I have organized my narrative into the life stories of five successive ancestors whose fates and values shaped the lives of their children. My story begins with the life and times of three men, Jonas Griffin (1762–1815), his son Francis Griffin (1800-1865), and his son Judge John Bettis Griffin (1826–1903). It ends with portraits of two remarkable women, Judge John's daughters, Mary Lane Griffin (1858–1942) and Helen Knight Griffin (1864–1949), my namesakes, Mimi and Nellie. The stories of these five people capture the early history of the Mississippi Delta, Warren and Washington Counties, and the town of Greenville.

SECTION ONE
JONAS GRIFFIN (1762–1815)

Descendants of Jonas (John Jones) Griffin

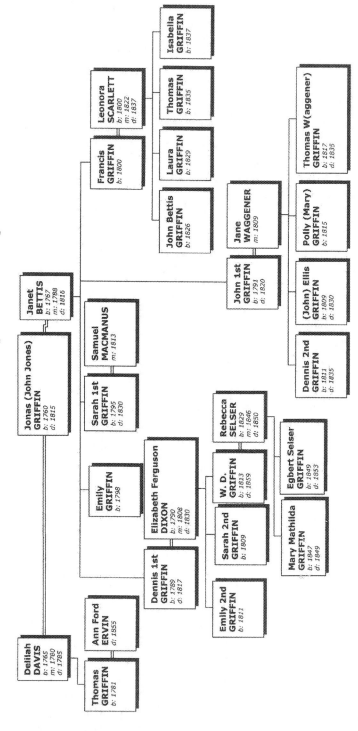

Chapter 1: A Pioneer Goes to the Wilderness

The first of my Griffin ancestors to settle in Mississippi were Jonas (1762–1815) and Janet (1766–1818), formerly Bettis, who were married in Cumberland County, North Carolina in 1788. The family genealogist and historian Lydia Griffin Trenholm could not trace Jonas before his marriage to Janet. She and others who have tried to take the Mississippi Griffin line back to the first Griffin who set foot on American soil have been frustrated by competing given names and a casual approach to record keeping. In 1910, for example, Carrie Stern read a paper to the Washington County Mississippi Historical Society in which she referred to Jonas Griffin, my great-great-great-grandfather, as Jeremiah Jonas Griffin. The Bettis family tree which carefully traces the descendants of Jonas' and Janet's son, Francis Griffin (1800–1865), refers to Jonas as Josiah in one place and as John in another. In her later years his great-granddaughter called him Jeremiah Josiah. Most Mississippi land and census records call him Jonas Griffin. Jonas, himself, complicated matters by changing the name he used on legal documents in South Carolina and Mississippi.

I have cobbled together a likely, though by no means certain, record of Jonas' ancestry by examining family trees and early legal records. His first American forbearer was probably a Jonas Griffin, son of Edward, who was born in Wales in the early seventeenth century and sailed as an indentured servant from Bristol in the 1630s to Warrasquyouke Plantation (later Isle of Wight Plantation and later still Isle of Wight County) in Virginia to work on a tobacco farm. That first Jonas worked off his indentured service obligation and fathered a son named Andrew born in Isle of Wight County in 1643. Andrew married a Mary Heath in 1665, claimed by patent 195 acres in Isle of Wight, Virginia, in

1715, and died in 1724. His son Matthew married a girl named Catherine Jones (1705–1755) in South Hampton, Virginia, and they settled, at least temporarily, in North Carolina, for one of their four sons, John Jones Griffin, who used his mother's maiden name in legal records, was born in Edgecombe County, North Carolina on June 1, 1735. Mathew later returned to Virginia where his will was probated in South Hampton following his death in 1751. Jones Griffin, his son, remained in Edgecombe County and married Martha, also named Jones, on April 27, 1761. Edgecombe County records also reveal that Jones Griffin—when he was thirty in 1765—sold land to his brother Andrew, who was named for an uncle and grandfather. Perhaps this was a portion of land Jones inherited from his father Matthew. Jones Griffin died in Edgecombe County in 1796 where his will listed three sons, John, Dempsey, and Francis.

Jones and Martha Griffin named their first son John Jones echoing both his father's full name and his mother's maiden name and called him John to distinguish him from his father, Jones. At the early age of eighteen, in 1780, John (no mention of Jones in the marriage record) Griffin married Delilah Davis of Edgecombe County. They soon had a son named Thomas and migrated to South Carolina where the 1784 tax list shows that John, now calling himself Jonas, owned two hundred and fifty acres and seven slaves. He probably followed his father's lead in adopting his middle name (Jones) as his first name. Perhaps the compiler of the tax list interpreted the "e" as an "a" to produce Jonas, or perhaps Jones decided to establish a new identity for himself, by choice or necessity, in South Carolina. Sometime between 1784 and 1788, Delilah disappeared from the records. She must have died, leaving Jonas without a wife to care for their young son and work on the farm. In 1788, when he was twenty-six, Jonas returned to Cumberland County, North Carolina and married Janet Bettis who was twenty-two. The couple returned to South Carolina where, in 1790, Jonas witnessed a land sale in the Orangeburg District of Winton County (later two separate counties, Orangeburg and Barnwell). While raising her eight-year-old stepson Thomas, Janet Bettis Griffin bore five more children: Dennis (1789–1817), John (1791–1821), Sarah (1795–1824), Emily (b.1797), and Francis (1800–1865). The 1800 United States Census shows Jonas living in Barnwell, South Carolina with a wife, one boy between sixteen and twenty (Thomas), two boys between six and sixteen (Dennis and John), two girls under six (Sarah and Emily), and one infant boy (Francis). Jonas and Janet chose names with family connections for their boys. John was named for his paternal grandfather, John Jones Griffin and, indeed, for his father. Dennis was named for a Carolina relative. Francis, the newborn, was named for his father's brother, Francis Griffin, and his mother's father, Francis Bettis.

A paper trail of land transactions shows how Jonas' growing ambition led him and his family to the Mississippi Territory. On April 26, 1797, when he was thirty-five, Jonas purchased two hundred acres of land on the Savannah River in nearby Edgefield County, South Carolina, for eight hundred dollars. He was expanding his holdings probably with money he inherited from his father in 1796. Then Jonas set his sights higher and further away. He left his land and family under the care of his seventeen-year-old son Thomas and set off alone on a grueling journey to the Mississippi Territory where it had become possible to claim tracts of virgin land. He found a tract of land south of what is now Vicksburg in Warren County, Mississippi, claimed it "by occupancy," and received a U.S. land patent. Such freeholds were generally offered in amounts of one hundred acres for each head of household and fifty acres for each member of the household (Morris 1995, 8). Since Jonas had six in his household, his wife and five children, he was eligible to claim a freehold of four hundred acres. The first reliable land records, which date from 1806, nine years after Jonas' original claim, list Jonas as both the current and original owner of plat #221 which was 630 acres, not four hundred. By 1806 Jonas had acquired a nearby plat #223, which consisted of 370 acres, from its original owner/claimant, Ambrose McDonald, who also paid Jonas one hundred dollars. The agreement for this transfer of land and money, presumably in settlement of a debt, is dated March 12, 1804, signed by Ambrose McDonald, and witnessed by Jonas Griffin and his neighbors Joseph Ferguson and Joseph Ferguson, Jr. Two years after arriving on the Delta in 1802, Jonas had expanded his original holding by more than half (*Transcriptions of Natchez Land Records*).

Mystery enters the picture with the intervening plat #222 of 334 acres. The name of the original claimant in 1797 was Jeremiah Jones, and that name appears as the owner in the 1806 Federal Land Office Registry. By that date, Jonas Griffin was also farming those acres. There may have been a real Jeremiah Jones, perhaps Jonas' uncle or a first cousin, who accompanied him to Mississippi to stake out the claim. Or perhaps Jonas simply invented the name to increase his holdings which may explain his later identification as Jeremiah. The original claim and the 1806 registration are the only appearances of Jeremiah Jones in the early records of Mississippi. Early Mississippi settlers needed more than the legal allotment of land to make farming cotton profitable, and they used various strategies to acquire additional acreage. Jonas Griffin seems to have taken advantage of the confused state of record keeping and the absence of personal identification to acquire 1,334 acres, a sizeable holding. The 1806 Land Office document gives the location of Jonas' claim as Smith Creek. That name has disappeared, but Smith Creek must have been a small tributary of the Homochitto River. Later documents indicate Jonas' land bordered that river which flows into the Mississippi just south of Vicksburg.

On his first trip to the Mississippi Territory, Jonas traveled northwest over the Carolina mountains, probably on Daniel Boone's Wilderness Road which had opened thirty years earlier.

In 1796, the Kentucky legislature decreed the Wilderness Road, at that time passable only on foot or by horseback and pack animals, should become an "all weather road." By 1797 it accommodated oxcarts and mule-drawn hogsheads. Once over the mountains, Jonas may have made his way first by horseback and then six hundred miles by canoe as did Josiah Gibson, a Methodist minister who traveled in 1799 from North Carolina to his new assignment in the Mississippi Territory (*BHMM*). More likely, he boarded one of the large flatboats that meandered down the Tennessee and Cumberland Rivers to the Ohio River, then to the Mississippi River, and on down to the Mississippi Territory. If he was frugal and adventurous, he might have hired on to man one of the six oars used to steer those heavily loaded lumberyards around obstacles, rapids, and snags as they floated with the current.

The flatboat trip was an adventure. Timothy Flint, a Methodist circuit rider, remarked it was "no uncommon spectacle to see a large family, old and young, servants, hogs" on a flatboat "bringing to recollection the cargo of the ancient ark." Indeed, these awkward boats were christened by newspaper wags of the time "Kentucky arks" (Van Every 1986). The oddity of the passengers and cargo was overshadowed by the dangers along the water's edge. Eager to trade, Indians became testy when no exchange goods were available. Pirates attacked the unwary or enticed crews into grog shops and ransacked the boats in their absence.

Between December 1797 and August 1799, the Harpe Gang—two brothers and their three wives—terrorized river traffic in Kentucky, Ohio, and Tennessee. Not content with robbery, the gang killed and disfigured their victims, often filling their body cavities with stones and sinking them in the river. They claimed thirty victims—including babies and children—during their two-year rampage. A posse (there were no organized police or militia to keep order in the wilderness) finally hunted the brothers down, ambushed them, and shot and decapitated Big

Harpe. The triumphant posse mounted his head on a stake by the river bank to warn other pirates. Newspapers as far away as Charleston, South Carolina featured the event (Rothert 1995, 101).

After registering his claim in Mississippi, Jonas bought a horse and rode the Natchez Trace from Natchez, Mississippi up into Tennessee through miles of Indian country claimed by the peaceful Choctaw and Chickasaws. John L Swaney, a post rider from 1796 to 1804, made the round trip from Nashville to Natchez and back to Nashville—about a thousand miles—every three weeks. He rode fifty-five miles a day and took a day's rest at each end of his route. On the Trace, Swaney met Indians, a few white settlers dispersed at forty-mile intervals, boatmen on their way north, and, perhaps, George Mason and his gang of "gentlemanly" highwaymen who never shed blood unless forced to. A clever robber with a Spanish passport, Mason carefully preyed only on U.S. citizens, and he often crossed the Mississippi River into Spanish territory to avoid pursuit. By 1803, he had a price on his head, a militia in pursuit, and a posse surrounding him. Two members of the posse captured Mason, cut off his head, covered it in blue clay to preserve it, and tramped into Natchez to claim their reward. When they were recognized as members of Mason's gang, citizens tried, convicted, beheaded, and buried them beside the Natchez Trace (Rothert 1995, 252).

At the end of the Trace near Nashville, Jonas either picked up the Wilderness Road or followed the riverbanks into South Carolina where, no doubt, he said several good Methodist prayers of thanksgiving for his safe return to his wife and six children. Several years later, in 1802, Jonas and Janet, their five children, and John's son, Thomas, a young man of twenty-one, retraced Jonas' exploratory trip to the Mississippi Territory. Recent improvements enabled them to haul their possessions and provisions through the mountains of Carolina into Tennessee in wheeled hogsheads or wagons. In eastern Tennessee they purchased a flatboat whose boards and logs they used to build a cabin at the end of their journey. Flatboats offered an essential source of finished boards. A sawmill was not built in the Vicksburg area until 1807 (Morris 1995).

Like other migrating families, the Griffins packed their flatboat with supplies to create a self-sufficient homestead: an ax or two, a planting spike, seeds, a plow, a mule, some pots and pans, one or two dressers or chests, some chairs, perhaps a spinning wheel, a musket, some corn, a cow, and some pigs. Since Jonas could read and write and Thomas would soon begin to preach in Methodist meetings, they also packed a Bible and some other books. In 1774, the going price for a boat big enough to carry a family, a wagon and four horses was $40. In 1783 Simon Kenton oversaw the building of a flatboat large enough to accommodate forty one people and nineteen horses. Its price must have been substantially more than most. According to an Ohio River traffic census of 1786, the average flat boat carried a cargo of 18 people and 13 head of stock (Van Every 1986, 34–5).

Since they were traveling thirty years after the first flatboats plied the Tennessee River, we can imagine the Griffins floated in a medium-sized craft about twelve feet wide and fifty feet long with side railings and a cabin divided into chambers provided with fireplaces. For protection against Indians and pirates, Jonas sought the company of other families moving down river in flatboats. With hired oarsmen who knew the river, families set off in a caravan that pulled in at night during stretches where it was shallow or rough. They traded with Indians and scared off pirates. Their destination was a substantial piece of land on the banks of Smith Creek six miles south of present-day Vicksburg in what became in 1809 Warren County. What Janet and Jonas accomplished in the next thirteen years attests to their strength of mind and body, their resilience, and their determination to create a better life for themselves and their children. They could not have ventured so far and struggled against such odds without the physical and moral support of Jonas' grown son Thomas. The family held high hopes and were proud to be at the forefront of the young country's efforts to settle and stabilize its western frontier.

Chapter 2: Life in the Mississippi Territory, 1800–1827

When Jonas decided to claim a large piece of virgin land in Mississippi and move his family there under hazardous conditions, he intended to plant it in cotton, buy slaves to work it, move into large-scale farming, and make a fortune. Extraordinary profits could be made from cotton since Eli Whitney's invention of the cotton gin enabled one person to separate as much lint from seed as twelve people could by hand. When the family arrived, they picked a spot on the bluffs above the Mississippi for their future home and began clearing the land. Vegetable gardens were a first priority, and it did not take them long to slash and burn six or seven acres around their cabin site to plant the corn, peas, and squash seeds and the fruit pits they brought from South Carolina (Morris 1995, 11). Until their garden began to produce they purchased staples from neighbors and lived off the land. Chickens brought by boat and purchased locally provided both meat and eggs. In the early nineteenth century, the Mississippi wilderness offered both food and income. Free-range pigs were a plentiful source of meat and meat products, and they could be sold to a nearby army encampment either on the hoof or smoked (Morris 1995, 30). Other wild game roaming the woods provided more meat, and the hides could be bartered or sold for cash. Harriet Blanton Theobold told the story of a pioneer housewife, "heroic and muscular," who saw a bear raiding her hen coop. "She took a hand spike and with five blows killed the brute at the gate" (McCain 1954, 52). Acorns and nuts were an abundant source of food for humans and animals. Early settlers called their settlement, which would become Vicksburg, Walnut Hills because walnut trees grew so abundantly (Rowland 1907). Game, native fruit, and, yes, mosquitoes were plentiful.

A high priority for the Griffins was building a place to live. The first Griffin house was a log cabin constructed from trees felled in the dense hardwood forests that covered the bluffs overlooking the Mississippi River. Like other settlers, the Griffins salvaged planed boards from their flatboat and transported them to their building site for a foundation, internal partitions, floors, and a roof. Jonas and Thomas may have hauled boards and felled and prepared trees fast enough to have a house-raising within a month of their arrival. Other families in the neighborhood helped the Griffins position their logs and raise a roof. Susan Dabney Smedes' grandfather, Colonel Thomas Dabney, settled in Mississippi in 1820. She wrote "it was the custom of small farmers to assist each other when one of them built a house." After receiving an invitation one day from a newcomer to help him raise his house, Colonel Dabney appeared with 20 slaves and did not leave until the log cabin was complete. He was surprised to learn later that his neighbor was offended by his use of slaves. On another occasion, he helped a neighbor whose cotton fields were "deep in grass." That man's response was equally surprising to Colonel Dabney: "if Colonel Dabney had taken hold of a plough and worked by his side he would have been glad to have his help, but to see him sitting up on his horse with his gloves on directing his Negroes how to work was not to his taste" (Smedes 1981, 53). Differences in class, background, and customs among early settlers of the Mississippi delta were not slow to emerge.

In 1802, there were no grand planters like Colonel Dabney. Natchez, a town seventy-five miles south of the Griffin property, contained only ten log dwellings. The Griffin men with help from neighbors built a simple one-story log cabin. The "grand house" built later to adorn the plantation they named Magnolia Terrace was only a two-story log cabin that resembled one described by Louis Hughes who came as a slave to a plantation carved out of the wilderness many years later in Pontotoc, Mississippi. It had two large rooms on each side of a long open hallway that ran from front to back. There were eight rooms, four downstairs and four up. The wide hallway served as public space and was fitted out with chairs and tables. The house had been chinked and plastered and whitewashed (Hughes 1897).

Frazer Smith carefully details how pioneer cabins evolved into dogtrot log houses during the nineteenth century in the new Southwest. He explains how their basic plan became that of the "plantation mansion."

> From the start, "some pioneers prospered more than others, and these promptly sought to provide extra comforts for their families. . . . A kitchen, a dining room, and even a parlor appeared in due time to enrich the social, religious, and certainly the matrimonial prospects of the family. However, the typical dogtrot plan was never discarded; it was simply enlarged by adding another story. The house was still built of hewn logs fitted together after the fashion of a log cabin. Two rooms faced the front with a wide (first open, then enclosed) hallway which housed the stairway. The plan of the second floor was the same as that of the first. A porch of medium width spanned the front of the house. This porch might be one or two stories high and was usually covered with a slanting roof. A single gabled roof crowned the main structure, and the hand-split shingles were fastened in place by wooden pegs. There was a stone chimney at each end of the house. A kitchen was often appended as an L to the rear, and as the family grew, the house grew, other rooms being similarly added (Smith 1941, 26–7).

By 1810 a sawmill had opened in Walnut Hills which enabled the planters to add board siding and cypress floors to their original log dwellings. When they accumulated enough capital, they ordered windows and doors from carpenters in New Orleans. Ample porches across the front and the back offered additional sheltered living and lounging space.

Harriet Blanton Theobold described a house built by William Blanton in Washington County in 1820:

> It was a double log house, with a broad hall, a great hospitable chimney, and a wide porch. This porch was the storing place for tools and saddles, stores as well, and soon gained the name of 'store house' which it never afterwards lost. There was a rail fence of about three or four rails high about the clearing.... This first house deserves special mention. Besides sheltering the family, it was the only stopping place for land hunters and travelers across the country. It was also the meeting house. For years a faithful circuit rider held services in it (McCain 1954, 51–2).

At a meeting of the Washington County Historical Society in 1910, Gracia Walton reported that Fredrick Turnbull, a Princeton College graduate, brought his wife and children in 1826 to live in two log cabins chinked with mud and white washed with a hall running between. This log house on the shore of Lake Washington "with broad piazzas front and back" was "the genesis of Linden," one of the most "delightful and hospitable houses in the state" (McCain 1954, 128). Those beautiful large houses came later. The cabin into which Janet Bettis Griffin moved her children made great demands on her ingenuity and patience; travelers and neighbors probably made equal demands on her larder. To Janet, who had been married in 1788 at the age of twenty two and was thirty six with five young children in 1802, the task of carving a home out of the humid wilds must have seemed overwhelming.

In *Becoming Southern,* Christopher Morris argues that the area around Vicksburg in the early nineteenth century was very like the frontier in Ohio and Indiana. Nuclear families came—or quickly formed—to undertake self-sufficient farming, supplementing their income from hunting, fishing, and trapping. As more settlers came, the forest resources dwindled, giving way to cultivation of cotton. With the advent of cotton, individual landowners increased their holdings. As they acquired more land, they acquired more slaves to work it. Vast differences in income and political power developed between those who owned large plantations worked by slave labor and those who did not. In the space of two decades, roughly 1800 to 1820, according to Morris, "a loosely knit, typically Western community of pioneer homesteaders [was transformed] into a distinctly Southern society based on plantation agriculture, slavery, and a patriarchal social order." This was precisely the period in which Jonas was acquiring more land to increase his capacity for cotton production. By 1815 he was poised to step from the rough-and-ready American West he helped tame into the rarified and privileged world of a Delta planter.

Even as pioneer farmers, Jonas and Thomas Griffin were active in their community. Jonas donated money for the first Methodist church building in the area, and he gave the land on which the church was built. Thomas served as Treasurer of Warren County for a brief period in 1807. Sometime in his early or mid-twenties, Thomas began preaching as a layman. Dunbar Rowland describes him as an eloquent preacher. Throughout the Mississippi Territory on several Sunday mornings each month, Methodist congregations without ordained ministers depended on laymen for their sermons. Perhaps as often as once a month they enjoyed the presence of a bachelor circuit rider who, if not yet ordained, was sanctioned by the Mississippi Methodist Conference. That body officially "received" Thomas Griffin, who was twenty-nine years old, as a circuit riding minister in 1809. Family circumstances probably delayed his decision until that year. His half-brother Dennis, now twenty, had married a year earlier and continued to live with his wife on Magnolia Plantation. Another half-brother John was eighteen in 1809. Both young men were able to take over the work Thomas had done for their father.

Having received a higher calling, Thomas felt free to leave Magnolia Terrace. In 1813 he was one of eleven delegates to the first annual meeting of the Mississippi Conference of the Methodist Episcopal Church. Over the years, he became a popular preacher on the Ouachita Circuit that included some settlements across the Mississippi River in Louisiana and some in northern Mississippi and Alabama near the Tombigbee River. For many years he remained a bachelor, depending on the kindness of his congregations for food and lodging. An early chronicler who knew Thomas described him as "an able and zealous man, well-fitted for his work."

> He had no education and was poor, but he studied by the campfire and the forest path, and he mastered the hardy elements of frontier life. In 1820 he represented Mississippi in the General Conference and was not pleased with certain expressions of Northern delegates, or the defensive attitude of those of the South. He made a speech which was not lacking in energy of expression. "It appears," said he, "some of our Northern brethren are willing to see us damned, double damned, rammed, jammed, and crammed into a forty-six pounder, and touched off into eternity" (Rowland 1907, Volume 2, 225).

In 1832, at the advanced age of fifty-two, Thomas Griffin married Ann Ervin, the widow of Hugh Ervin, and the daughter of John Ford, an established Methodist minister. The Conference of the Methodist Episcopal Church then assigned Thomas to a fixed ministry in Madison County, Mississippi, where he acquired a plantation and slaves, prospered, and fathered several children.

The Spartan conditions of life in the early Mississippi Territory took their toll. Family legend had Jonas living to a "ripe old age," but that was not the case. His dream of becoming a wealthy planter ended abruptly in 1815 when at the age of fifty-three he died. A year later, in 1816, his widow Janet shared with her four surviving children—Dennis, John, Sarah, and Francis—a portion of her father Francis Bettis's estate when he died in North Carolina. But she was no longer a member of the Griffin household in the 1820 Census which means she died sometime between 1816 and 1820, probably from yellow fever during the epidemic of 1818. Her daughter Emily, who would have been nineteen years old in 1815, was also dead since she is not mentioned in her father's will, that of her grandfather, or the 1820 Census. Yellow fever is the most likely culprit in all three Griffin deaths. In 1818, the Reverend Newit Vick and his wife, both of Warrenton, died from yellow fever leaving twelve children under the age of nineteen (*BHMM*, Volume 2, Part 2, 957). Mosquitoes thrived in the hot humid climate, and no one knew they were spreading the dread disease.

By tracing the fate of Janet and Jonas Griffin's children, we can see how their youngest child, Francis, who was an infant when they arrived in Mississippi, became at a very young age the head of the Griffin family and principal heir to their substantial holdings. On July 20, 1808, Francis' older brother Dennis, who was nineteen, married Elizabeth Dixon in Wilkinson County a hundred miles south of Warren County. Since in family lore, Dennis married an Elizabeth Ferguson, the woman he married must have been a Ferguson who married a Dixon, moved south, and then became a widow. Elizabeth was probably the daughter of Joseph Ferguson Sr. and the sister of Joseph Ferguson, Jr. neighbors who signed the document that transferred the land claim of Ambrose McDonald to Jonas Griffin 1802. Dennis and Elizabeth must have been childhood friends.

Since Dennis and his new family continued to live on Magnolia Terrace or on a nearby Ferguson plantation he was able to assist his father in managing his holdings. Two years after his father died, however, in 1817 when he was only twenty-eight, Dennis died, having named his brother Francis, who was only seventeen, guardian of his three young children—Emily (age eight), Sarah (six), and young Dennis (four) who was called W.D. to distinguish him from his father. Not long after she was widowed, on March 3, 1817, Elizabeth Dixon Griffin, no doubt an attractive woman, married Colonel William Rushing, a Warren County landowner. He soon replaced Francis as the guardian of Elizabeth's children and the administrator of her husband's estate.

Janet and Jonas' second son, John Griffin, married Jane Waggoner from Amite County, Mississippi, in 1809 when he was eighteen. They had four children: Ellis, born in 1809 and probably named John Ellis after his father, but called Ellis to avoid confusion; Dennis, born in 1811 and named in enduring Griffin tradition for his father's older brother; Thomas, born in 1813 and named for his maternal grandfather and his father's half-brother; and Polly (more formally Mary) who was born in 1815. In the 1820 Census, Jane Waggoner Griffin had become Head of Household on her father's plantation in Amite County many miles southeast of Warren County. There is no mention of her husband John who must have been yet another Griffin victim of the 1818 yellow fever epidemic. When her father, Thomas Waggoner, died in 1824, his daughter Jane and her four children are listed among his heirs.

Jonas and Janet Griffin's surviving daughter Sarah, who was born in 1795, five years before Francis, married Samuel MacManus on April 10, 1813 when she was eighteen. The young MacManuses lived with his parents in Woodville, a town thirty miles south of Walnut Hills between Warrenton and Natchez. According to the 1820 Census, they had two boys and one girl all under ten. By 1830, Sarah, who would have been thirty-five and one of her two boys were no longer members of Samuel McManus's household; presumably they were dead.

Marriage, probate, and Census records demonstrate how Jonas and his three sons moved from the role of pioneer farmer to that of cotton planter. In 1800 Jonas Griffin—still in South Carolina—owned no slaves. In 1810, in Mississippi, he owned five. Five years after he died, the 1820 Census shows Francis on Magnolia Terrace owning sixteen slaves. Jonas' older sons married young women whose fathers owned both land and slaves. Along the banks of the Mississippi River, the pixie dust of a careful marriage transformed many a pioneer holding into a small cotton kingdom. Neighbors encouraged (if they did not arrange) marriages between their sons and daughters to consolidate their holdings and bring more fertile farmland under their purview. Summer heat and humidity sapped energy and bred mosquitoes. They in turn spread yellow fever. Disease and death reshaped families and brought ever-larger tracts of land under the control of a single planter. A wife left with small children needed a man, ideally a new husband, to manage her property. When a well-to-do grandfather died in a more settled part of the country, he left something for his daughter and grandchildren. Second marriages following the death of spouses combined small holdings into larger holdings. Relatives and guardians used this land and other family resources they controlled, often temporarily, for collateral to secure credit and to purchase more land and slaves.

At a very young age Francis Griffin assumed responsibility for his brother Dennis's young children and managed his affairs for a few years. He then did the same for the young family of his brother John following his early death. In a country, without a government welfare system, family members were expected to care

19

for each other and did so. At a very young age, Francis also became the principal heir to the holdings Jonas Griffin had carved out of the wilderness and transformed into Magnolia Terrace. Jonas' efforts to become a grand planter were truncated by death. Other deaths decimated his family with the result that his youngest son, Francis, who was only a small baby when his parents transplanted him to the Mississippi Territory, became the sole surviving heir of his father and went on to realize his father's dream.

Chapter 3: From Mississippi Territory to Southern Slave State

Jonas Griffin and his pioneer neighbors came to the wilderness of the Mississippi Territory and lived in egalitarian, frontier communities. These first Mississippi immigrants settled widely separated delta areas, one along the east bank of the Mississippi River above New Orleans and the other along the Tombigbee River above Mobile. The great tracts of the Choctaw and Chickasaw Indian Nations divided the two halves of the Mississippi Territory. The slender chain of the Natchez Trace offered the only safe-passage roadway through Indian Territory between Nashville and Natchez. Francis Griffin grew up while the Territory transformed itself from a frontier into a full-blown patriarchal plantation society in one generation.

Cheap land, easy credit, and an explosion of technology fueled the shift, but slavery propelled it. When statehood came in 1817 many foresaw slow economic growth. They underestimated the siren song of cotton and the force of human greed. Profitably cultivating cotton demanded a large readily available labor force. The cotton-growing South chose chattel slavery based on race to supply it. The institution of slavery collided with the rule of law and the culture of honor. The collision changed Mississippians' beliefs about law, honor, race, and slavery itself. The progress was steady. By 1859 the citizens of Mississippi viewed the world very differently from their northern counterparts.

Law in the early days of the Territory resembled our American myth of the taming of the West. In countless movies of the last century, law in the guise of the United States Marshal arrived in a lawless cow town. The terrified citizens welcomed him as a savior from outlaws carrying guns. With one or two spectacular gun battles, the Marshal cleaned up the town; the citizens elected a sheriff; banditry and vigilante justice were no more. Imposition of law in the Mississippi Territory did not move so smoothly. In 1798 Winthrop Sargent, from Massachusetts, came to govern a wilderness without roads, towns, or any written laws. His executive journals preserved in the *Mississippi Territorial Archives* reveal his difficulties in setting up a territorial government. The United States Congress had sent him three Federal Judges without legal training, and they had failed to bring law books. Governor Sargent had counted on using the laws of existing states as models for Mississippi law. Two of the three judges were so unhappy in the wilderness of Mississippi that they soon decamped to South Carolina. Undaunted and pragmatic, Governor Sargent promulgated laws himself, divided the Territory into two counties, and appointed a citizen board (Board of Quorum) to act as the executive and judicial body of each county. In 1799 the Counties of Adams and Jefferson (called Pickering at the time) stretched from the Mississippi River on the west across what is now Alabama to the boundary of the State of Georgia on the east. Two boards of five men governed the entire area. As each new county was created, the governor appointed a five-man Board of Quorum for it. As I have said, Jonas Griffin served on the first Board of Quorum in Warren County. This system of appointed boards governed counties for nineteen years until Mississippi became a state in 1817. The sparsely populated Territory developed a frontier independence matched by an idiosyncratic application of law. In *Becoming Southern* Christopher Morris argued that many years of rule by Boards of Quorum shaped citizens' attitude toward the law even after they began to vote for county officers. Planter-patriarch society, during the first half of the nineteenth century, preferred to decide matters of justice by consensus. Men worked out an agreement and then brought that agreement to the courthouse for a stamp of approval. In isolated interdependent neighborhoods consensus often prevailed over the letter of the law.

Morris demonstrated how custom trumped written law in Mississippi as late as 1836. He made his point with the curious case of the Widow Griffin of Warren County who was not, to my disappointment, a member of my Griffin family. Her husband, Furney, homesteaded north of Magnolia Terrace. He had the bad luck to sell a portion of his original 1797 claim to Malachi Gibson in 1806. By 1836 the widow, Keziah Griffin, lived on a farm in the Walnut Hills area surrounded by land owned by various members of the wealthy Gibson clan. Keziah's horse wandered into a Gibson field and was shot. When her hogs trespassed, Levi Gibson "had his overseer chase them away with hounds that relished the taste of bacon. He and his kin persisted in using a short-cut between their plantations ... until they had worn a road through [Keziah's] field." The *Vicksburg Advocate and Register* reported Mrs. Griffin as saying Levi Gibson "need not be surprised if he found a thousand dollar Negro dead on the road some time or other." In August a dead slave turned up in the lane, and Keziah received a visit. The Gibsons and their friends came to her house, threatened her, and she "fled" with her daughter across the river to her kin in Louisiana. Time passed. Belatedly, Levi Gibson seemed to worry about public opinion and his honor. He published a notice in the Vicksburg newspaper which began: "This publication is to show the cause for the expelling of Mrs. Griffin and family from the neighborhood." The Griffins filed suit against Levi Gibson, and the case dragged on for five years as witnesses for the Griffins failed to appear. But in the end, the Griffins prevailed and won $6,000 in damages. Morris concluded that in the community's eyes Levi Gibson had violated his patriarchal responsibility of leadership and protection of the weak. "It is significant that law and the court provided justice only when local male leaders came to the Griffins' aid, moved by a sense of paternalistic duty" (Morris 1995, 99–100).

The long rule of Boards of Quorum led Mississippi citizens to devalue the letter of the law, and the institution of slavery reinforced that devaluation. It created a tier of residents to whom laws did not apply. The Mississippi legislature and Mississippi courts struggled to come to terms with the fact that slaves, before the law, were both persons and property. Only in criminal cases were slaves granted rights generally accorded to persons. "Slaves were rarely sent to jail, the punishment for non-capital offenses took the form of whippings (thirty-nine lashes 'well-laid on'), branding, or the cutting off an ear" (Lang 1977, 106). On the plantation, the master was the law for his slaves. In civil cases, however, slaves were "a species of property common in this country." Not only could they be sold "absolutely or conditionally," they could be "mortgaged, levied upon by creditors, recovered in actions of *detinue* and *replevin,* made the subject of larceny, and made the *res* for trusts. They could be hired for a term, be bequeathed for life and in remainder, warranted for title and soundness, and held as tenants in common. In short ... there were virtually no limitations on the right to acquire, hold, or dispose of slaves on whatever terms the parties chose" (Lang 1977, 49–50).

When Jonas and his fellow pioneers came to Mississippi, they were likely to see slavery not as a positive good, but a necessary evil. Misgivings about slavery emerge in the document organizing the territory. It gave the General Assembly full power to "prevent slaves being brought into this state as merchandise." The framers of this document envisioned a pattern of settlement similar to that of Ohio or Kentucky. Economic growth might be slow, but slave labor would be rare. A few farmers might use slaves to clear and farm their newly claimed land, but most families would farm small plots with hired labor when needed. A few planters might march slaves they already owned overland from Virginia or South Carolina or ship them in flatboats through Kentucky and Tennessee. After the State Constitutional Convention in 1817, however, the Legislature neglected to exercise its power to prohibit in-state slave trade. In *Defender of the Faith*, Meredith Lang reported a "staggering" growth in the slave population in

Mississippi from 33,000 in 1820, to 65,000 in 1840, to over 195,000 in 1840. By 1830 Mississippi had entered "flush times." Natchez was home to more than twenty millionaires whose fortunes were based on cotton, and the town had a thriving and notorious slave market.

Flush times in the new South (Mississippi, Louisiana, and Alabama) began as planters in the old South realized their slave populations exceeded their need for labor. Virginia and the Carolinas contained fewer large tracts of land to clear and plant. Tobacco, the traditional cash crop of the piedmont, required much less labor than cotton. Planters in the old south were unwilling to solve their excess labor problem by sending their slaves to colonize Liberia. Neither the federal government nor any state government was willing to sell publicly owned land to finance emancipation and transportation to Africa. In 1832 the Virginia Legislature rejected a proposal to emancipate and export all slaves to Africa. In 1840, the same body rejected Thomas Jefferson Randolph's proposal to make all slaves born after 1840 the property of the state and enable them to work on public projects to defray the cost of transporting themselves to Africa. As their slave populations grew too large, slave owners in the old south began to view their slaves as a profitable commodity. Planters could make good money by selling them to speculators and traders for transport to the new South and the labor-hungry cotton economy (Gudmestad 2005). By 1840 the ratio of slaves to citizens was five to one in many cotton-producing counties in Mississippi. By 1854, the ratio of slaves to citizens in Washington County was ten to one.

As the number of slaves grew within the state, the courts and the Mississippi legislature began to articulate state policies to limit the number of slaves within the state and then the number of free Negroes. In May 1833 the Legislature, at last, exercised its right to "prevent slaves from being brought into this state as merchandise."

The Courts began to hold contracts negotiated in Natchez for the sales of slaves "void as against public policy." Soon appeals to the United States Supreme Court reversed the Mississippi High Court findings. Until that reversal, the "Natchez" slave market moved across the state line into Louisiana, and traders drew up contracts in West Feliciana Parish. Between 1837 and 1842 the Mississippi Legislature enacted a number of statutes to govern the sale of slaves within the state and to prohibit the emancipation of slaves within the borders of Mississippi. All wills that emancipated slaves at their master's death were declared void by an act in 1842. Seventeen years later, in 1859, the Mississippi High Court held "Mississippi and other states, under the firm conviction that the relationship between master and slave, which has existed within her limits from the organization of the state government to this day, is mutually productive of happiness and the best interests of both, continues the institution and desires to perpetuate it. She is unwilling to extend to the slave race freedom and equality of rights or to elevate them into political association with the family of States" (Lang 1977, 90–1).

We have seen how isolation and slavery undercut the rule of law during the first half of the nineteenth century in Mississippi. Another element of Southern culture played an essential role. In the twenty-first century the word "honor" sounds old-fashioned. We seldom use it outside the Marine hymn or the Boy Scout pledge, but honor was a real force in patriarchal plantation society. Recent historians have shown how the uneasy coexistence of honor and slavery conditioned and distorted Mississippians' perceptions. The highest concern for men of honor, according to Kenneth Greenberg, was their public reputation among their equals. Long after dueling had disappeared from the Atlantic states and prohibitions against dueling had been written into law in the Southern states, fighting words still occasioned duels in Mississippi. Many Mississippians shared the view expressed by William Gilmore Simms: the man of honor "fights to maintain his position in society, to silence insult, to check brutality, prevent encroachment, and avenge a wrong of some sort and in obedience to fierce passions that will not let him sleep under the sense of injury and annoyance" (Greenberg 1996, 14).

Southern "men of honor" demonstrated power, generosity, and a disdain for mere possessions by lavish hospitality to friends. They gave extravagant Christmas gifts to their families and to their slaves. They willingly cosigned for large debts. They gambled for high stakes. They even burnished their honor by running for public office. By dueling, they demonstrated their courage and their disdain for preserving life at the cost of honor. In Greenberg's reading of the language of honor, the duel is the extreme "gift" to heal a "breach" in society: "The central purpose of the duel was not to kill, but be threatened by death. Hence the exchange of shots on the dueling ground should be thought of as a double gift exchange. Each man shot a bullet and gave his adversary a chance to demonstrate that he did not fear death; honor was more important than life. Each man allowed his adversary to shoot at him, and therefore paid him the compliment of acknowledging his social equality" (1996, 74). This description makes honor sound like a virtue, but honor, when it collided with slavery, became a vice.

Men of honor all-too-often enlarged their own sense of honor by denying it to others—women, slaves, freedmen, strangers, professional gamblers, slave traders, and abolitionists (Greenberg 1996, 137). Slaves had no honor because they had nothing of their own to risk or give. They could be legally whipped and stripped by their masters. Professional gamblers mocked men of honor who believed the best gamble was one that risked everything. While men of honor played to demonstrate their honor, professional gamblers played to win. Strangers traded for profit without regard for the personal circumstances of their customers. Dishonorable

Doctor Thomas Beall. Beall threatened Selser with a pistol and W.D. stepped between them, whereupon Beall stabbed W. D. and shot Selser. Both died on the spot. This was no weekend drunken brawl by riverboat ruffians. The two victims were successful cotton planters from the area below Walnut Hills. Newspapers all over the country printed the story. Benjamin Wailes, another Warren County planter, who was vacationing in Philadelphia at the time, wrote in his diary, "I saw in a Philadelphia paper an account of the killing of Doct. Selser & W.D. Griffin at Warrenton, Mississippi by a Doct. Beall which appears to be a brutal assassination. . . . The character of Mississippi and Warren County is likely to have an infamous notoriety" (Olsen 2000, 170).

It is hard to tell if Wailes was more upset over the double murder or the fact newspapers outside of Mississippi printed the story. When I first read about the event, I assumed adultery or perhaps a heated political difference had precipitated the murder. Further research unearthed the truth. George Selser had stained the honor of Dr. Thomas Beall by refusing to allow him to court his sister. Quite possibly lubricated with bourbon, Beall had his revenge. He asserted and defended his honor by killing two men on the sidewalk in Warrenton. Selser was his main target, but he may not have minded killing his defender as well. Thirteen years earlier W.D. Griffin, a fellow planter, had measured up to Selser's standards and married another of his sisters, Rebecca, on April 21, 1846.

Dr. Beall was arraigned for murder; the 1860 Census lists him as a resident of the Vicksburg jail. His trial ended with a hung jury, and he was released (Morris 1995, 97, 229; Olsen 2000, 170). Some members of the jury, probably not members of the planter class, sympathized with Beall. His honor had been dealt a blow that deserved satisfaction. Perhaps Beall had challenged Selser to a duel which Selser, a member in good standing of planter society, had refused. Even if Selser was not opposed to dueling,